My Walk Scavenger Hunt

Bela Davis

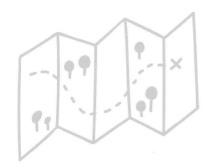

Abdo Kids Junior
is an Imprint of Abdo Kids
abdobooks.com

Abdo
SENSES SCAVENGER HUNT
Kids

abdobooks.com

Published by Abdo Kids, a division of ABDO, P.O. Box 398166, Minneapolis, Minnesota 55439.
Copyright © 2023 by Abdo Consulting Group, Inc. International copyrights reserved in all countries.
No part of this book may be reproduced in any form without written permission from the publisher.
Abdo Kids Junior™ is a trademark and logo of Abdo Kids.

Printed in the United States of America, North Mankato, Minnesota.

052022

092022

THIS BOOK CONTAINS
RECYCLED MATERIALS

Photo Credits: Getty Images, Shutterstock

Production Contributors: Teddy Borth, Jennie Forsberg, Grace Hansen

Design Contributors: Candice Keimig, Pakou Moua

Library of Congress Control Number: 2021950541

Publisher's Cataloging-in-Publication Data

Names: Davis, Bela, author.

Title: My walk scavenger hunt / by Bela Davis.

Description: Minneapolis, Minnesota : Abdo Kids, 2023 | Series: Senses scavenger hunt | Includes online
    resources and index.

Identifiers: ISBN 9781098261580 (lib. bdg.) | ISBN 9781644948392 (pbk.) | ISBN 9781098262426
    (ebook) | ISBN 9781098262846 (Read-to-Me ebook)

Subjects: LCSH: Senses and sensation--Juvenile literature. | Walking--Juvenile literature. | Scavenger
    hunting--Juvenile literature.

Classification: DDC 612.8--dc23

Table of Contents

Walk Scavenger Hunt

Let's go on a hunt! Can we find these things on a walk?

1 small animal - - - - - - - - - - - - - - - - - -

2 wood wall - - - - - - - - - - - - - - - - - -

3 bike sound - - - - - - - - - - - - - - - - - -

4 colored door - - - - - - - - - - - - - - - - - -

5 sweet treat - - - - - - - - - - - - - - - - - -

6 flower smell - - - - - - - - - - - - - - - - - -

We have five **senses**. They can help find things.

I see with my eye.

I see small dogs.

I feel with my hand. I feel a wood fence.

I hear with my ear.

I hear a kid on a bike.

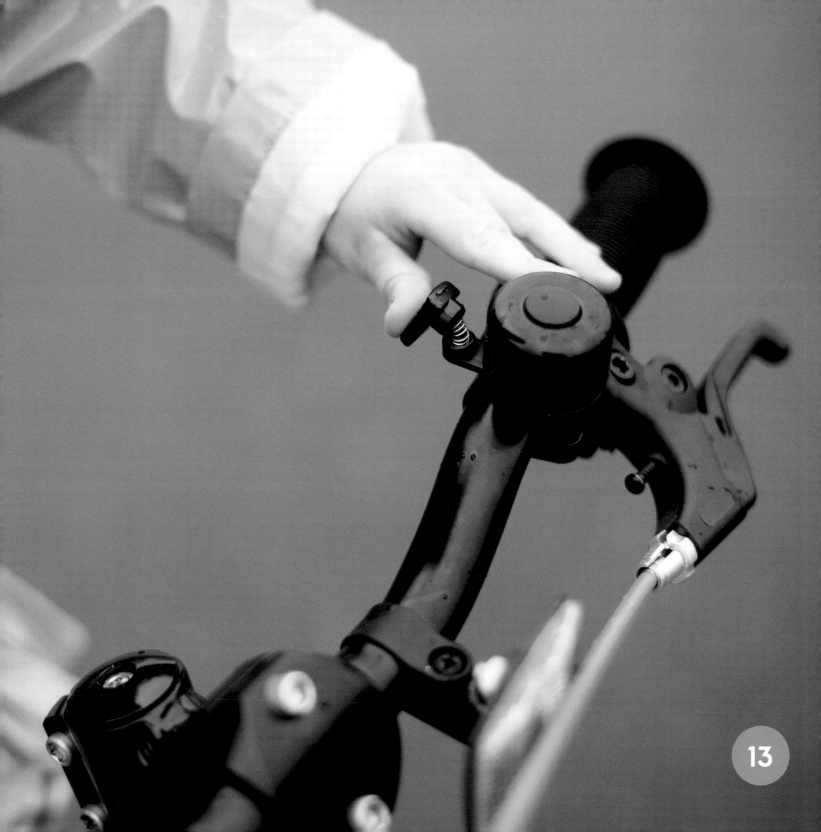

I see with my eye.

I see a blue door.

I taste with my tongue.

I taste a lollipop.

I smell with my nose. I smell a tree in **bloom**.

We found all 6 things! Can you find them on your walk? Happy hunting!

Make Your Own Scavenger Hunt

Decide Where to Go

Make a List of Things
You May Find

Add Senses to That List

Find Your Things!

Glossary

bloom

the state or time of being in flower or producing flowers.

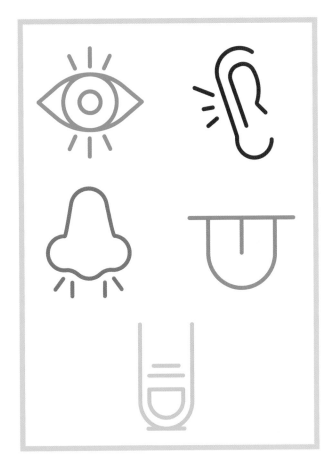

sense

any of five ways to experience one's surroundings. The senses are sight, hearing, smell, taste, and touch.

Index